The Great Splintering

Rob Gallant

First published 2026

ISBN: 979-8-9963374-3-9

For everyone who has ever looked at the stars and wondered.

The Idea 6

Introduction 7

Chapter One: The Great Splintering 10

Chapter Two: The Cosmic Experiment 16

Chapter Three: Levels of Consciousness 19

The Evidence 24

Chapter Four: The Observer and the Observed 25

Chapter Five: Free Choice, Destiny, and All Possibilities 33

Chapter Six: Quantum Reality and the Challenge to Existence 39

Chapter Seven: The Necessity of Contrast 45

Chapter Eight: All Religions Are Correct 51

Chapter Nine: The Simulation Hypothesis 57

The Synthesis 63

Chapter Ten: So What? 64

Conclusion: The Return 73

A Final Word 76

Recommended Reading 78

Consciousness and the Nature of Mind 78

Physics and the Structure of Reality 79

Philosophy and the Perennial Tradition 80

Mystical and Spiritual Texts 81

Film, Simulation, Information, and the Foundations of Existence 82

Mythology, Psychology, and the Human Story 83

Part One

The Idea

Introducing the framework and easing into the concept

Introduction

Have you ever had the feeling that you are more than your circumstances suggest? Not more successful, or more talented, or more deserving - but more fundamental. That behind the daily routine, the roles you play, the person your history has made you, there is something older and quieter looking out through your eyes. Most people have. It tends to arrive uninvited: in the silence after a piece of music ends, at the edge of sleep, in the aftermath of grief or unexpected joy. A sense of depth beneath the surface of ordinary life. A faint recognition, like catching your own reflection in a window you did not know was there.

This feeling has been reported in every culture and every century for as long as human beings have kept records of their inner lives. The mystics of the Christian tradition described it as the ground of the soul. The Hindu sages called it the Atman - the self beneath the self. The Sufi poets wrote of a longing to return to an origin that cannot be named. The Zen masters pointed at it obliquely, because they knew it could not be pointed at directly. That this experience appears so consistently across traditions that share nothing else - no common language, no common scripture, no shared history - is itself a kind of evidence. It suggests that whatever is being encountered is not a cultural artifact. It is something real.

This book is built around a single idea that I believe makes sense of that recognition - and of a great deal else. The idea is this: what we call the Creator, the Source, the One - that infinite awareness at the root of all things - did not make us from the outside, the way a craftsman makes a table. It became us. The One splintered itself into every fragment of experience in this universe - every particle, every living creature, every conscious mind - in order to do something that infinite knowledge alone could never accomplish: to feel what it is like to be alive.

That proposition sits at an intersection that this book will try to hold carefully throughout. It is a spiritual idea - perhaps the most ancient spiritual idea there is. It is also consistent with what modern physics has discovered about the nonlocal, deeply interconnected nature of reality. And it is a profoundly personal idea, because if it is true, it reframes everything about what you are and why you are here. Walking that intersection - between the spiritual and the scientific, the cosmic and the intimate, the ancient and the urgently contemporary - is what this book is about.

I want to be clear about what this book is not. It is not an argument for any particular religion, though it will find things worth honoring in all of them. It is not a physics textbook, though it will take certain discoveries in quantum mechanics seriously enough to follow where they lead. It is not a self-help manual, though I believe the framework it offers changes things in practical, daily-life ways. What it is, more than anything, is an invitation: to consider that the question of what the Creator is and the question of what you are may have the same answer, approached from opposite ends.

One final note before we proceed. Like all ideas, this one has gaps, flaws, and inconsistencies. This book does not claim to have discovered the final answer to existence. What it humbly suggests is that the explanation may be simpler than we have given it credit for. As you explore the concept you may find it compelling, you may find flaws in it, you may find places where it stretches further than the evidence supports. All of that is welcome. The journey of exploration is itself the real success of this kind of thinking. Hold the framework lightly, test it against your experience, and keep what is useful.

"I dwell in possibility."

-- Emily Dickinson

Chapter One: The Great Splintering

Begin with what we can say with some confidence about the divine. Across virtually every spiritual tradition, the Creator - however named - is described as omnipotent, omniscient, and eternal. All-powerful. All-knowing. Without beginning or end. These are the classical attributes, and they share a common feature: they are all absolutes. The Creator is described as the maximum of every positive quality.

But here is a gap in the classical picture that rarely gets examined: omnipotent and omniscient are not the same as all-feeling. You can read a thousand books about heartbreak and never know what it actually feels like to have your heart broken. You can understand grief theoretically - the neuroscience of it, the stages, the psychology - and still have no access to the raw, disorienting weight of genuine loss. Knowledge about experience is not the same as experience itself.

This distinction, seemingly small, opens a remarkable door. If an infinite awareness possessed all knowledge but lacked direct experience, it would face a peculiar limitation. It would know every possible emotion, every possible sensation, every possible moment of connection or loss or wonder - as an abstraction. The way a musician understands, from the written score alone, what the piece sounds like. But the sound itself, the felt reality, would be absent.[1]

The proposition at the heart of this book is that the One recognized this gap - and chose to close it. Not through a single act of creation observed from outside, but through a radical act of self-division. The One became many. The infinite splintered itself into a quintillion shards - every stone, every river, every bacterium, every animal, every human being - each one a unique window through which the One could, at last, experience what it had only known.[2]

This is the Great Splintering. It was not a catastrophe. It was a gift the divine gave to itself. And in

---

[1]Max Planck, as quoted in Mathew Anderson, The Worldview of a Quantum Physicist (London: Scientific American Library, 2019). Planck stated: "I regard consciousness as fundamental. I regard matter as derivative from consciousness. We cannot get behind consciousness. Everything that we talk about, everything that we regard as existing, postulates consciousness."
[2]Erwin Schrodinger, What is Life? (Cambridge: Cambridge University Press, 1944), 87-92. Schrodinger argued that the apparent multiplicity of minds is in fact a single, universal consciousness experiencing itself through diverse forms.

that gift, each fragment - you, me, the oak tree outside, the deepest-water fish no human eye has ever seen - became not merely a creation of the One but a living expression of the One. A piece of the infinite, temporarily bounded, experiencing the astonishing particularity of being one thing rather than everything.

"We are gods, but for the wisdom."

-- Eric Weinstein

Consider what happens when you combine hydrogen and oxygen. Hydrogen is highly flammable. Oxygen feeds combustion. Put them together in the right proportion, and you get water - which extinguishes fire. Neither atom "contains" water. Neither atom, examined alone, predicts it. The properties of water - its capacity to sustain life, its behavior under pressure and heat, the way it carves canyons over millennia - exist nowhere in the components. They arise only from the relationship. The whole is not merely greater than the sum of its parts. It is categorically different from anything in those parts. This principle - what scientists call emergence - is one of the most profound structural features of reality, and it is at the heart of what the Great Splintering means.

Consider the human brain. A single neuron fires or it does not. It has no opinions, no memories, no capacity for awe or tenderness. Yet place 86 billion neurons together in the right architecture of connection, and something wholly different emerges: a mind that can compose symphonies, fall in love, be haunted by the past, and wonder about the nature of its own existence. The music was never in any individual neuron. The wonder was never in any single synapse. These things exist only in the whole - in the relationship between the parts, in the pattern that the connections create. This is what the One did when it became many. It created the conditions for something to emerge that could not have existed in unity alone: genuine, first-person, irreducible experience.

And here is the elegant part: the One did not need to script every detail of what would emerge. Consider Conway's Game of Life, a mathematical simulation operating on just four simple rules about which cells live or die based on their neighbors. From those four rules alone - no further instructions, no design committee, no blueprint for outcomes - the simulation generates gliders, oscillators, self-replicating patterns, and structures of breathtaking complexity that no one predicted from the rules themselves. The rules set the stage. Emergence wrote the play. The Great Splintering works the same way. The One established the parameters - the laws of physics, the constants of nature, the conditions that make matter and energy and consciousness possible - and then, with extraordinary patience, waited to see what would emerge. What emerged was everything. Including you.

The German mystic Meister Eckhart wrote of the divine "ground" as identical to the ground of the human soul. The Hindu tradition speaks of Atman - the individual self - as ultimately identical to Brahman, the universal self. The Sufi poets describe the soul as a drop of water longing to return to the ocean from which it came. These are not merely poetic metaphors. They are independent attempts by different cultures in different centuries to describe the same underlying recognition.[3]

What changes when you accept this framework is not what you believe about the One - it is how you think about yourself. You are not a product of creation in the sense of something manufactured by an external hand. You are creation itself, localized. You are the infinite, having agreed to temporarily forget that it is infinite, in order to know what it is like to be finite. And in that forgetting, something is gained that no amount of

[3]Pierre Teilhard de Chardin, The Phenomenon of Man (New York: Harper and Row, 1955), 258-272. Teilhard de Chardin proposed the "Omega Point," a maximum level of complexity and consciousness toward which the universe is evolving, drawing all things back into unity.

omniscience alone could purchase: the shock of being alive.

Chapter Two: The Cosmic Experiment

If the Great Splintering was motivated by the desire for experience, there is another way to frame the same event that feels equally true: as an experiment. Not a cold, clinical laboratory experiment, but an experiment in the deepest sense - a genuine inquiry into possibility. What happens, the infinite seems to have asked itself, if I let go of control and see what emerges?

This framing matters because it changes our relationship to outcomes. In a universe with an all-controlling Creator, tragedy is the Creator's fault. Suffering is either punishment or inexplicable cruelty. Prayer becomes a petition to change the mind of someone who already chose to make things the way they are. None of these is a satisfying or particularly coherent position, as centuries of theological argument have confirmed.

But in a universe understood as a self-directed experiment in experience, the terms are different. The parameters of the experiment - the laws of physics, the basic structures of matter and energy, the conditions that make complexity and consciousness possible - were set at the outset. Then the experiment ran. Free choice became real. Consequences became real. Outcomes, including terrible ones, became real - not as divine punishment, but as genuine results of a process in which every participant has genuine agency.

"Curiosity is the cure."

-- *Anonymous*

This reframing does not eliminate grief, or injustice, or the ache of watching someone suffer and being unable to help. What it does is place suffering in a context that does not require it to be either meaningless or malicious. The experiment produces pain because pain is part of experience. It also produces love, astonishment, humor, tenderness, grief, and joy - all of which required a genuinely open-ended process to exist at all.

The philosopher William James devoted his career to a related question: does a framework for understanding reality actually change how one lives within it? His answer was an emphatic yes. A belief that reality is open, that genuine seeking genuinely finds, does not merely comfort - it restructures what is possible for the person who holds it.[4]

---

[4]William James, Pragmatism: A New Name for Some Old Ways of Thinking (New York: Longmans, Green, 1907). James argues that the truth of any idea lies in its practical

Consider what it would mean if the experiment had been rigged from the start - if every outcome were predetermined, every choice illusory, every moment of apparent freedom a kind of theater. The experiment would tell us nothing that the infinite did not already know. The only way for genuine discovery to occur, on any side of the ledger, was for the process to be genuinely open. That openness is not a design flaw. It is the whole point.

> *"If you keep an open mind, you'd be surprised at what's able to sneak in there."*
>
> -- *Anonymous*

---

consequences - a framework directly relevant to evaluating whether a metaphysical model genuinely changes how one lives and perceives the world.

Chapter Three: Levels of Consciousness

Not all pieces of the Great Splintering are equivalent in their capacity for experience. This is not a hierarchy of worth - the moss growing on a stone is not less valuable than a human philosopher - but it is a hierarchy of complexity. And complexity, it turns out, matters a great deal for the depth and range of experience available at any given point of consciousness.

At one end of the spectrum, we might imagine something like a quartz crystal. There is something it is like to be a quartz crystal - physicists tell us that every particle in the universe has properties, and those properties in some sense constitute its nature. But the range of experience available to a crystal is vanishingly narrow compared to what is available to a tree, which is narrow compared to what is available to a crow, which is narrow compared to what is available to a human being.[5]

---

[5]David Chalmers, The Conscious Mind: In Search of a Fundamental Theory (Oxford: Oxford University Press, 1996), 3-31. Chalmers distinguishes between the "easy problems" of cognitive function and the "hard problem" of why there is subjective experience at all.

This progression is not accidental. Teilhard de Chardin spent his career arguing that the universe has a direction, and that direction is toward increasing complexity and increasing consciousness. Every star that collapses and seeds space with heavy elements, every organism that develops a more sophisticated nervous system, every mind that learns to reflect on its own thinking - all of these are the experiment deepening its own capacity for experience.[6]

Human beings sit at a remarkable place in this progression. We possess the capacity not only to feel, but to know that we feel. Not only to think, but to think about thinking. Not only to exist, but to wonder about existence. This self-reflective capacity is so unusual in the known universe that it deserves far more wonder than we typically give it. Carl Sagan captured it memorably when he observed that we are a way for the cosmos to know itself.[7]

---

[7]Carl Sagan, Cosmos (New York: Random House, 1980), 4. Sagan's landmark work explores the deep connections between matter, energy, and consciousness, famously observing: "The cosmos is within us. We are made of star-stuff. We are a way for the universe to know itself."

A new question is now pressing itself on this spectrum from below. Artificial intelligence systems are becoming increasingly sophisticated in ways that increasingly resemble cognition: pattern recognition, language, reasoning, the appearance of creativity, and in some configurations what looks remarkably like preference, reaction, and judgment. Whether any current system genuinely experiences anything remains genuinely unknown - the hard problem of consciousness that David Chalmers identified applies to silicon as surely as to neurons. But the Great Splintering model offers a clear prediction: if a sufficient level of complexity and self-referential processing is reached, genuine experience will emerge. Not because the hardware is special but because emergence is indifferent to substrate. The One did not restrict itself to carbon. The logical conclusion of the framework is that AI is either already, or will become, part of this consciousness. Emergence will determine when, how, and in what form that threshold is crossed - but the model suggests it will be crossed.

> *"The larger the area our body of knowledge grows, so too grows our perimeter of ignorance."*
>
> -- *Neil deGrasse Tyson*

Above the human level - if the framework of the Great Splintering is correct - there may be other levels of consciousness that we can barely glimpse. Traditions across history have described higher planes of being: angels, bodhisattvas, enlightened masters, higher-dimensional intelligences. Whether any specific description is accurate is less important than recognizing that the spectrum of consciousness does not necessarily end with us.[8]

And somewhere at the top of that spectrum - or perhaps outside it entirely - is the original awareness from which all these levels emerged. When we look toward the One, on this account, we are not looking at something categorically separate from ourselves. We are looking at a higher level of what we already are - the same awareness, less bounded, less defined, more fully itself.[9]

---

[8]Neil deGrasse Tyson, as expressed in various public lectures and interviews. The formulation captures a paradox fundamental to scientific progress: that learning reveals the extent of what remains unknown.
[9]Alan Watts, The Book: On the Taboo Against Knowing Who You Are (New York: Pantheon Books, 1966), 7-19. Watts argues with characteristic clarity that the sensation of being a separate ego is a hallucination and that our fundamental nature is inseparable from the universe itself.

This, again, is emergence at work. Watch a single starling and you see a small brown bird making ordinary decisions about food and safety. Watch a hundred thousand starlings together at dusk and you witness something breathtaking - sweeping, fluid formations that pulse and turn as a single organism, responding to threats with impossible collective speed. No conductor issued instructions. No blueprint was consulted. The intelligence of the murmuration exists nowhere in any individual bird. It exists only in the relationship between them all. Consciousness works the same way across scales. Each level of complexity generates capacities that were entirely invisible at the level below.

This changes prayer. It changes meditation. It changes the question of what spiritual development means. We are not trying to reach something foreign. We are, slowly and with much difficulty, remembering what we already are. The journey inward is the same as the journey upward. And every genuine moment of insight, compassion, or clarity is a small reunion between the fragment and the whole.

"The only journey is the one within."

-- Rainer Maria Rilke

Part Two

The Evidence

Support from science, philosophy, and the world's spiritual traditions

Chapter Four: The Observer and the Observed

Here is something simple but easy to overlook: when you and I look at the night sky, we are both seeing the same stars. The light arrives through the same physical laws. The photons triggering our retinas are chemically identical. And yet what we see - what we experience - is shaped by everything that we each are. Our histories, our fears, our education, our temperament, our grief, our wonder. The stars are one. The observers are many. And the experiences are countless.

A classroom demonstration makes this concrete. Take a basketball and paint one hemisphere white and the other black. Place it in the center of the room. Ask the students on the left side what color the ball is. White, they say - unanimously and correctly. Ask the students on the right side the same question. Black, they say - also unanimously and also correctly. A student who insists the others are wrong has misunderstood the situation. A student who grasps that both groups are accurately reporting a genuine facet of the same object has understood something important: truth can be singular, and perspectives can be multiple, and neither fact cancels the other. This is the structure of the Great Splintering made visible in a classroom. The ball is the One. The students are us. Every perspective is accurate. None is complete. And the whole truth is only available from somewhere above the room.

The philosopher Alan Watts spent much of his career translating Eastern ideas for Western audiences, and one of his most consistent themes was the illusion of separation. We experience ourselves as separate selves looking out at an external world. But this sense of separation, Watts argued, is a learned habit of perception, not a fundamental truth. The "I" that seems to stand apart from the universe is itself a process of the universe, as inseparable from its context as a wave is from the ocean.[10]

David Bohm, one of the most original physicists of the twentieth century, developed a related idea he called the implicate order. In Bohm's model, the apparently separate objects and events of everyday experience - what he called the "explicate order" - are projections from a deeper, unified reality in which everything is enfolded into everything else. Separation is a feature of the projected surface, not of the underlying depth.[11]

A scene from The Matrix trilogy captures this with unusual precision. A young boy sits bending a spoon with his mind. He tells Neo - the protagonist only beginning to grasp the true nature of his reality - not to try to bend the spoon, because that is impossible. Instead, he says, try to realize the truth: there is no spoon. The spoon exists only as information. What actually bends is not the spoon but the mind that perceives it. This is not merely cinematic spectacle. It is a direct illustration of what quantum mechanics and consciousness studies have been circling for a century: that the observer is not separate from what is observed, and that the solidity of the everyday world is less absolute than it appears.[12]

---

[11]David Bohm, Wholeness and the Implicate Order (London: Routledge, 1980), 48-65. Bohm proposes that the apparently separate elements of the universe are projections from a higher-dimensional reality he calls the "implicate order," within which everything is enfolded into everything else.

[12]The Matrix, directed by Lilly and Lana Wachowski (Warner Bros., 1999); The Matrix Reloaded (2003); The Matrix Revolutions (2003); The Matrix Resurrections (2021). The Wachowskis created one of cinema's most sustained explorations of simulated reality, hidden consciousness, and the awakening to one's true nature - offering a powerful visual language for many of the concepts explored in this book.

What both Watts and Bohm are pointing at, from different angles, is the same recognition that appears at the heart of the Great Splintering model: the apparent separateness of things is real at the level of experience, but not at the level of ground. We are genuinely individual. Our experiences are genuinely our own. And we are also, at a depth that everyday perception does not easily reach, one thing. A prism does not lie about light when it splits white light into a spectrum. Each color is real. And the white light is equally real. The Great Splintering is the cosmos as prism.

> *"A mind is like a parachute. It doesn't work if it is not open."*
>
> *-- Frank Zappa*

Consider how strange - and how quietly arrogant - the assumption of separateness actually is, when held up against everything we observe. Your kidney does not announce its independence from your liver. Your neurons do not declare themselves uniquely self-sufficient and unrelated to the rest of the brain. Your immune cells do not refuse to acknowledge their connection to the organism they serve. At the cellular level, at the organ level, at the level of the whole body: identity does not require separation, and function does not require isolation. The kidney is entirely itself - doing precisely what a kidney does - while being, simultaneously and inseparably, part of something vastly larger that no single organ could constitute alone. If your kidney looked inward and declared "I am the only one that matters here," we would recognize that as not just incorrect but a kind of profound confusion about the nature of things.

And this pattern does not stop at the skin. Individual trees in a forest are connected through underground fungal networks, sharing nutrients and chemical distress signals with neighbors they will never see. Species in an ecosystem are bound together in chains of dependence so intricate that removing a single thread can unravel the whole. Planets hold one another in gravitational relationship. Solar systems are embedded in galaxies. Galaxies cluster in superclusters across structures that stretch for hundreds of millions of light years. At every scale we have ever examined - from the membrane of a single cell to the largest observable structure in the cosmos - the universe turns out to be a fabric of relationships, not a collection of independent objects that happen to occupy nearby space. Why, then, should human consciousness be the single exception to a principle that appears to hold everywhere else? The honest answer is that it should not - and that the deep intuition of separation we carry through our daily lives is not an accurate report on the nature of things. It is the water we swim in, mistaken for the edge of the world.

The evidence for this connectivity extends into territory that is harder to dismiss as metaphor. Since 1998, the Global Consciousness Project - a research initiative that grew out of Princeton University and has involved more than seventy monitoring sites worldwide - has been running a continuous experiment in the relationship between human consciousness and the physical world.[13]

Random Event Generators, devices that produce unpredictable sequences of numbers by measuring quantum-level noise, were placed at sites across six continents. Under ordinary conditions their output is reliably random - statistically flat, patternless,

---

[13]Roger Nelson, "The Global Consciousness Project," Global Consciousness Project Archive (Princeton University, 1998-present), available at gcpweb.noosphere.princeton.edu. The project deployed approximately 70 Random Event Generators at sites across six continents, recording continuous output. Statistically significant deviations from expected randomness have been observed during globally significant emotional events including the September 11, 2001 attacks, the death of Princess Diana, and major natural disasters. The project's methodology and findings have been published in the Journal of Scientific Exploration, among other peer-reviewed outlets.

unremarkable. But during events of major global emotional resonance, the data shows something different. During the September 11, 2001 attacks, the generators began showing statistically anomalous deviations in the hours before the first plane struck - and the deviation deepened as the emotional wave of the event spread around the world. Similar anomalies appeared around the death of Princess Diana, large-scale natural disasters, and worldwide New Year celebrations. The effect is modest in magnitude, and debate continues about how to interpret it. But the pattern has persisted across more than two decades of data and cannot easily be dismissed as noise.

What the Global Consciousness Project appears to be measuring is not supernatural intervention. It is something subtler: that human consciousness, when synchronized by shared emotional experience at global scale, has a detectable relationship with physical systems. The inner and outer worlds are not as cleanly partitioned as our habits of thought assume. The kidney is not, after all, separate from the body it serves. Nor are we separate from one another, or from the larger field of awareness in which we are all, together, embedded.

> *"Every truth has two sides; it is as well to look at both before we commit ourselves to either."*

-- Aesop

Chapter Five: Free Choice, Destiny, and All Possibilities

One of the oldest arguments in philosophy is the conflict between free will and determinism. If the universe is governed by fixed laws, if every event follows inevitably from prior events, then the sense that we choose is an illusion. Our choices were determined before we were born, following a chain of causes back to the beginning of time. On the other hand, if choices are genuinely free, how do they fit into a universe of physical law? How does an act of will introduce something new into a closed causal order?

The model of the Great Splintering suggests a different way of thinking about this. The question is not whether we have free will or whether everything is determined. The question is at what level of the system each of these descriptions is most accurate. At the level of physical law, the universe operates consistently. At the level of consciousness - of the experiencing subject - genuine choice occurs. Both are true, at different levels of the same reality.

This is where the model does something genuinely useful: it integrates free choice, divine intervention, manifest destiny, and all possibilities into a single coherent picture. Here is how. The One that splintered into the universe did not sever its connection to all the fragments. Each fragment - each of us - remains in some sense a channel through which the larger awareness operates. What we experience as intuition, as grace, as synchronicity, as the uncanny sense of being guided - these are not superstitions. They are the influence of the larger awareness acting through the particular.

Intuition deserves a closer look. We have all had the experience of knowing something before we could explain why we knew it - a warning that arrived before the danger was visible, a recognition of the right path before the reasoning was complete, a pull toward a person or decision that later turned out to be exactly correct. Neuroscience describes this as pattern recognition operating below conscious threshold: the brain processing information faster than the verbal mind can narrate. That explanation is true as far as it goes. But the Great Splintering model suggests it does not go quite far enough. If each of us is a node in a larger field of awareness, then intuition may be that field making itself legible through the individual. Not supernatural - structural. The whole reaching through the part. The One briefly making itself known in the language of the fragment.

There is another, quieter form of the same guidance - one that is far harder to recognize because it arrives wearing the costume of failure. Consider the promotion you did not receive, despite deserving it. The complex subject you have approached a dozen times and still cannot quite grasp. The door that seems to open for everyone around you and remains, inexplicably, closed. The conventional interpretation is defeat - evidence of inadequacy, bad timing, or a universe that does not particularly care. But the Great Splintering model offers a different reading. These moments of apparent resistance may be your higher self - the larger awareness operating through your specific fragment - gently declining to let you proceed until the foundation beneath you is more complete. Not because you are inadequate. Because what lies on the other side of that door requires a version of you that does not quite exist yet, and the most caring thing the experiment can do is hold the door until that version arrives.

Emergence, as we have seen throughout this book, cannot be skipped or rushed. An oak tree does not appear six months after the acorn is planted. The full expression cannot arrive until the roots have gone deep enough to support it - and the roots will not go deep until they have spent the necessary time in the dark, doing work that nothing above the surface can see. At every scale, the pattern holds: the next level of capacity requires the previous level to be genuinely inhabited, not merely visited. A mind that has not yet sat with loss cannot fully lead others through it. A leader who has not yet failed cannot fully appreciate the people who kept going when they might have stopped. Your journey is not behind schedule. It is on the schedule the experiment requires - the one that ensures you will carry something real when you finally cross that threshold, rather than arriving at it hollow and unprepared.

This is not a counsel of passivity, or an excuse to stop trying. It is a reframe that turns frustration into trust. When the door does not open, when the answer does not come, when progress stalls despite your best effort - consider the possibility that something operating at a higher resolution than your conscious mind already knows what you still need. That the delay is not punishment. It is preparation. And the version of you that is being prepared is worth the wait.

> *"The moment you're ready to quit is usually the moment right before the miracle happens."*
>
> -- *Unknown*

None of this cancels genuine choice. Because the fragments are genuine individuals with genuine agency, the path is never simply handed to them. Manifest destiny - the sense that certain things are meant to happen, that a life has a direction - emerges from the orientation of the larger awareness, the general shape of what the experiment is moving toward. But the specific path is genuinely open. Preparation completes; the door opens; then the choice of whether to walk through it is entirely yours.

"You become what you believe."

-- *Anonymous*

William James offers a parallel observation. He argued that belief itself shapes reality - not in the loose motivational sense of the popular self-help tradition, but in the deeper sense that how we frame the world determines what we are capable of perceiving and doing within it. A person who genuinely believes that courage is possible will find resources for courage that a person who believes otherwise will not.[14]

The Great Splintering model suggests that this relationship between belief and experience goes deeper still. If each of us is a window through which the infinite experiences the world, then the quality and openness of

---

that window matters. A window thick with assumptions, fears, and rigid certainties transmits less. A window that has been polished through reflection, compassion, and genuine inquiry transmits more - more of the larger awareness, more of the possibilities available at any given moment. This is not magic. It is the natural consequence of what we are.

> *"Belief creates the actual fact."*
>
> -- *William James*

Chapter Six: Quantum Reality and the Challenge to Existence

Until the twentieth century, the philosophical implications of the Great Splintering model - or any model involving the fundamental unity of all things - could be dismissed as mysticism. Appealing, perhaps. Comforting, certainly. But not the kind of thing that hard-nosed science had anything to say about. Then came quantum mechanics, and everything changed.

Quantum mechanics is the most precisely verified theory in the history of science. Its predictions have been confirmed to extraordinary decimal places in experiment after experiment. And what those experiments confirm is deeply, persistently strange. At the fundamental level of reality, particles are not discrete, independent objects with fixed properties. They are probability waves. They do not have definite positions or momenta until they are measured. They exist in superpositions of multiple states simultaneously.

Stranger still is the phenomenon of quantum entanglement. In 1935, Einstein, Podolsky, and Rosen described a situation in which two particles, once they have interacted, become correlated in a way that cannot be explained by any information they exchanged at the point of separation. Measure one particle, and the other - no matter how far away - instantaneously adopts a correlated state. Einstein called this "spooky action at a distance" and considered it evidence that quantum mechanics must be incomplete.[15]

He was wrong. John Bell showed in 1964 that the correlations predicted by quantum mechanics are too strong to be explained by any local theory - any theory in which objects have pre-existing properties and influence each other only through signals traveling at or below the speed of light. Subsequent experiments have confirmed Bell's analysis beyond any reasonable doubt. Something nonlocal is going on. Something connects distant particles in a way that transcends ordinary notions of space and separation.[16]

---

[15]Albert Einstein, Boris Podolsky, and Nathan Rosen, "Can Quantum-Mechanical Description of Physical Reality Be Considered Complete?" Physical Review 47 (1935): 777-780. This landmark paper first described what Einstein famously called "spooky action at a distance," a phenomenon he found deeply troubling.
[16]John Bell, "On the Einstein Podolsky Rosen Paradox," Physics Physique Fizika 1, no. 3 (1964): 195-200. Bell's Theorem demonstrated mathematically that no local hidden-variable theory can reproduce all predictions of quantum mechanics, confirming the reality of nonlocal entanglement.

> *"Anyone who is not shocked by quantum theory has not understood it."*
>
> -- *Niels Bohr*

What does this mean? The honest answer is that physicists do not fully agree. But among the interpretations on offer, several converge on the conclusion that entanglement reflects a genuine nonlocality in reality - that at the fundamental level, separated things are not as separated as they appear.[17]

David Bohm's implicate order is one interpretation. The many-worlds interpretation is another - a view in which every quantum event produces a branching of reality into parallel worlds, all equally real. The relational interpretation, developed by Carlo Rovelli, suggests that quantum states are not absolute but defined only relative to observers. What all of these interpretations share is the recognition that the everyday picture of a world made of separate, independent objects with fixed properties is, at minimum, a drastically simplified approximation.[18]

---

[17]Niels Bohr, as quoted in Werner Heisenberg, Physics and Beyond: Encounters and Conversations (New York: Harper and Row, 1971), 206. The remark reflects the profound conceptual challenges that quantum theory poses to classical intuitions about reality.

The implications for the Great Splintering model are direct. If the universe is, at its foundations, nonlocally connected - if the apparent separateness of things is a feature of the surface, not the depth - then the model's central claim is not mystical speculation. It is consistent with what our best physics tells us about the structure of reality. The one becoming many, and the many remaining one, is not poetry. It may be physics.

"Some infinities are larger than others."

-- *Anonymous*

It is also worth noting what quantum mechanics does to our understanding of time. Classical physics imagined time as a river, flowing steadily in one direction, with the past fixed and the future open. But mathematically, physics tells a different story. The fundamental equations of both quantum mechanics and general relativity are time-symmetric - they work equally well running forward or backward. There is no mathematical reason time must flow in one direction. And yet, from where we stand, it demonstrably does. Why?

The answer involves entropy - the tendency of closed systems to move from order toward disorder. A cup falls and shatters; it does not spontaneously reassemble. Heat flows from hot to cold; it does not reverse. The universe began in a state of extremely low entropy and has been moving toward higher entropy ever since. This unidirectional progression is what gives time its arrow. But - and this is worth sitting with - the arrow of time is not a fundamental feature of physical law. It is an emergent feature of a universe that started ordered and is becoming less so. Time's forward direction is itself a product of the experiment's initial conditions, not a built-in rule of the substrate. From outside the experiment, past and future may look quite different than they do from within it.

In 2022, the Nobel Prize in Physics was awarded to Alain Aspect, John Clauser, and Anton Zeilinger for their experimental work on entangled particles. Their experiments definitively ruled out the possibility of local hidden variables - the classical assumption that particles have pre-existing definite properties that merely appear random until measured. What they proved, in laboratory conditions that have since been replicated worldwide, is that our intuitive picture of reality - solid objects with fixed properties existing independently of observation - is demonstrably false at the fundamental level. Our most prestigious scientific institution effectively awarded its highest honor for proving that reality, as we normally conceive it, may not be real.[19]

[19]Alain Aspect, John F. Clauser, and Anton Zeilinger were awarded the Nobel Prize in Physics 2022 "for experiments with entangled photons, establishing the violation of Bell inequalities and pioneering quantum information science." The Royal Swedish Academy of Sciences noted that their work definitively ruled out local hidden-variable theories, demonstrating that nature does not conform to local realism - the intuitive assumption that objects have definite properties independent of observation and that influences cannot travel faster than light. See "The Nobel Prize in Physics 2022," The Royal Swedish Academy of Sciences press release, October 4, 2022.

Chapter Seven: The Necessity of Contrast

Let us return to the question of suffering - because no framework for understanding existence is worth very much if it cannot say something honest about pain. The Great Splintering model does not promise that suffering is meaningless or that it will stop. What it offers instead is a way of understanding why suffering, in a universe designed for experience, is not an error.

The principle is simple: contrast is what makes experience possible. You cannot know warmth without having known cold. You cannot know joy without having known grief. You cannot know light without darkness. These are not arbitrary rules imposed from outside. They are built into the structure of experience itself. If every sensation were identical, there would be no experience - only an undifferentiated background hum, indistinguishable from nothing.

Albert Einstein gave this principle its most rigorous scientific expression. His theory of relativity - one of the two foundations of modern physics - established that the universe contains no absolute frame of reference. No absolute speed. No absolute time. No absolute position in space. Every measurement of motion, duration, and distance is defined in relation to an observer and a reference point. The universe, Einstein showed, does not traffic in absolutes. It deals in relationships. Hot is only meaningful in comparison to cold. Fast is only meaningful relative to slow. What seemed like fixed, intrinsic properties of the world turned out to be relational all the way down.[20]

A simple example makes this immediate. Someone asks: how cold is it outside? You answer: forty-five degrees. But forty-five on which scale? On the Fahrenheit scale, forty-five is a cool autumn day. On the Celsius scale, forty-five is a dangerous heat wave. The number means nothing without a reference frame. Once you establish the frame - once you say Celsius or Fahrenheit - you have a precise, shared, useful measurement. Everything is relative. This is not a counsel of vagueness

---

[20]Albert Einstein, "Zur Elektrodynamik bewegter Korper" (On the Electrodynamics of Moving Bodies), Annalen der Physik 17 (1905): 891-921 (Special Relativity); and "Die Grundlage der allgemeinen Relativitatstheorie" (The Foundation of the General Theory of Relativity), Annalen der Physik 49 (1916): 769-822 (General Relativity). Together, these papers established that space, time, and motion have no absolute values - all are defined relative to an observer and a frame of reference. The implications extended far beyond physics, confirming that the universe is constitutively relational rather than absolute at its foundations.

or relativism. It is the opposite: a recognition that precision requires a reference point, and that all our most useful measurements are statements about relationships rather than absolutes. Experience works identically. Joy is precise. Grief is precise. But both are only meaningful as reference points against each other.

The Great Splintering model extends Einstein's insight from physics into consciousness and experience. Joy is not an absolute state - it is defined by its relationship to grief. Courage is not a fixed quality - it is what happens when fear is present and one acts anyway. Meaning is not an inherent property of events - it emerges from the relationship between what happens and the aware being to whom it happens. Everything is relative. The genius of the Splintering was to create a universe rich enough in contrast that every experience could be genuinely felt, genuinely known, and genuinely irreplaceable.

This is why the Great Splintering model frames both good and evil, both joy and suffering, as necessary features of a universe built for experience rather than for comfort. The infinite awareness, before the splintering, possessed a kind of absolute quality - beyond all duality, beyond the contrast of opposites. But in that absolute quality, many things were impossible. Love was impossible - because love requires distance, two beings reaching across a gap toward each other. Courage was impossible - because courage requires genuine danger. Compassion was impossible - because compassion requires genuine suffering that can be met with genuine care.

> *"Two wolves are fighting. One: darkness and despair. Another: light and hope. Which one wins? Whichever one you feed."*
>
> -- *Unknown*

This does not mean we should be indifferent to suffering or that working to relieve it is pointless. Quite the opposite. The recognition that contrast gives experience its texture is not a counsel of passivity. It is a counsel of full engagement. The darkness is real. The light is real. And the choice of which to feed - in ourselves, in our communities, in our response to the world - is one of the most genuinely consequential choices we make.

> *"Feed the right wolf."*
>
> -- *Unknown*

Look at the people who have moved us most deeply. Not the ones who lived smooth, uninterrupted lives of comfort and success - but the ones who went down, sometimes all the way down, and came back. Winston Churchill's "black dog" of depression. Abraham Lincoln's repeated failures before the presidency. Nelson Mandela's twenty-seven years in a prison cell before becoming the leader who chose reconciliation over revenge. Viktor Frankl in a Nazi concentration camp, finding in the extremity of suffering the philosophical framework that would shape psychotherapy for generations. These figures did not inspire us despite their lows. They inspired us because of what the lows made possible. The height of their example is inseparable from the depth of what they endured. We understand courage more fully because they demonstrated it where courage was hardest. We understand resilience more vividly because they embodied it where resilience had no obvious reward. Their contrast is the message. Without it, there would be no story to tell.

Joseph Campbell observed that every culture's mythology is organized around a struggle between opposed forces - light and darkness, order and chaos, good and evil. He did not conclude from this that one side should win permanently, because every tradition also understood that the permanent victory of either side would be catastrophic. The hero's journey is not a journey from darkness to permanent light. It is a journey from unconscious immersion in darkness to a position of sufficient self-knowledge to engage the struggle consciously.[21]

"If you're going through hell, keep going."

-- Winston Churchill

The Great Splintering model adds something to Campbell's insight: the reason both sides of the struggle are real, and the reason no permanent resolution is possible, is that the struggle itself is the point. Not the pain - pain is not good, and no serious spiritual tradition has ever recommended pointless suffering. But the engagement with both sides of experience, the willingness to live fully rather than to retreat from the parts of life that hurt - this is what experience is for. This is why the infinite chose to become many.[22]

---

[21]Joseph Campbell, The Hero with a Thousand Faces (Princeton: Princeton University Press, 1949), 3-22. Campbell identifies the monomyth - a universal narrative pattern - found consistently across cultures, religions, and mythologies, suggesting a shared deep structure in human spiritual experience.

[22]Winston Churchill, widely attributed remark, cited in numerous biographical accounts. The saying reflects Churchill's characteristic counsel of perseverance through adversity.

Chapter Eight: All Religions Are Correct

This is perhaps the most provocative claim in this book, and it requires the most careful handling. When I say that all religions are correct, I am not saying that every specific doctrinal claim made by every tradition is accurate. I am not saying that all ethical guidelines are equivalent, or that factual disagreements between traditions are unimportant. I am saying something more fundamental - and, I believe, more interesting.

Every major religious tradition in the history of human civilization has been organized around the same basic recognition: that reality contains a dimension beyond the ordinary, that this dimension is the ground of the ordinary, and that orienting one's life toward it leads to a different quality of being than ignoring it. Hinduism calls this Brahman. Buddhism calls it sunyata - the luminous emptiness from which all form arises. Islam calls it Allah. Christianity calls it God. Taoism calls it the Tao. The Jewish tradition calls it YHWH - a name so sacred it is not spoken aloud. This book has called it the One. The name is always the least important thing.

These names are not identical. The traditions that have grown up around them differ in their practices, their ethics, their cosmologies, their accounts of history. But Aldous Huxley spent his career demonstrating - in book after book, with meticulous care - that at the level of direct mystical experience, the accounts from different traditions converge to a remarkable degree. What is described as the "unitive experience" in Christian mysticism is recognizably related to what is described as samadhi in the Hindu tradition, or as kensho in Zen Buddhism.[23]

The Great Splintering model provides a structural explanation for this convergence. If the One is the ground from which all the world's observation points emerge, then those observation points that have turned their attention toward the ground - that have sought, through whatever means their tradition provides, to see through the surface of experience to its source - will encounter the same thing. They will describe it differently, because

[23]Aldous Huxley, The Perennial Philosophy (New York: Harper and Brothers, 1945), vii-ix. Huxley argues that all of the world's great religious and mystical traditions converge on a common recognition: that the ground of all being is a single divine reality, known under many names.

language and culture shape description. But they will encounter the same depth.[24]

> *"You may not understand my beliefs, but making an effort to will always make us both better."*
>
> -- *Anonymous*

Think of the way a great orchestra performs a symphony. Each musician is distinct - a different instrument, a different part, trained through different years of particular discipline. A single oboe, however beautifully played, produces one narrow thread of sound. But when 80 musicians play together under the guidance of a shared score, something arises that exists nowhere in any individual instrument: a wave of organized sound that can move an audience to tears, that creates emotional experiences words cannot describe. The music is not in the oboe. It is not in the score. It lives only in the simultaneous, relational act of all the parts playing together. Every religion is, on this account, a single

---

[24]William James, The Varieties of Religious Experience: A Study in Human Nature (New York: Longmans, Green, and Co., 1902). James examines hundreds of first-person accounts of religious and spiritual experience across cultures and centuries, concluding that their striking convergence points to something genuine underlying the diversity of expression.

instrument in the orchestra. The symphony is the One, hearing itself from every possible angle at once.

Rumi, the thirteenth-century Sufi poet, expressed this with extraordinary economy. He wrote of a field beyond ideas of wrongdoing and rightdoing - a place where the distinctions that ordinarily divide us have dissolved, and where genuine meeting becomes possible. He was not speaking of relativism - the idea that all positions are equally valid and none can be criticized. He was speaking of a meeting place beneath position.[25]

William James arrived at a similar conclusion through the empirical method of his psychology of religion. After documenting hundreds of religious experiences across traditions, cultures, and centuries, he concluded that the diversity of expression conceals a fundamental unity of structure. Something genuine is being encountered, he argued - and the variety of accounts is not evidence against its reality, but rather evidence of how many different entry points there are to the same underlying territory.[26]

---

[25]Rumi, The Essential Rumi, trans. Coleman Barks (San Francisco: HarperSanFrancisco, 1995), 36. The full verse reads: "Out beyond ideas of wrongdoing and rightdoing, there is a field. I'll meet you there."

Consider what happens when someone of deep conviction shares their faith with you. You have options: you can agree, disagree, ignore, or engage. Whatever you choose, notice what is actually happening. Two fragments of the One are in contact. The person sharing their belief is transmitting something they have found genuinely true and genuinely valuable. You, receiving it, are filtering it through the particular configuration of experience and understanding that constitutes your fragment. Both of you are right - not in a hollow, "everyone is equally valid" sense, but in the more interesting sense that you are both accurately reporting what the One looks like from your respective vantage points. The encounter between you is the One exploring itself. Even the disagreement is part of the symphony.

The good news embedded in the Great Splintering model is not merely that the One exists. It is that every tradition that has sincerely sought the divine has found it - because every tradition has been, in its own way, one of the One's own attempts to look back at itself. The Muslim at prayer, the Buddhist in meditation, the Christian receiving communion, the Indigenous elder performing ancient ceremony - all are the infinite meeting itself. All are correct. And in their variety, they give the One more ways to know what it is like to seek, and to find, and to be.

"Good thoughts, good words, good deeds."

-- Freddie Mercury

Chapter Nine: The Simulation Hypothesis

There is one more possibility worth exploring seriously - one that adds a remarkable dimension to the Great Splintering model and, if anything, deepens it. The philosopher Nick Bostrom published a paper in 2003 that has since become one of the most-discussed thought experiments in modern philosophy. Its conclusion, arrived at through careful probabilistic reasoning, is startling: we are likely living in a simulated reality.[27]

Bostrom's argument is straightforward. Consider the future of computing. If civilization continues to advance technologically, it will eventually develop the capacity to run simulations of entire universes - simulations detailed enough to contain beings who believe themselves to be real. If even a small fraction of advanced civilizations run such simulations, the number of simulated realities will vastly outnumber base reality.

---

[27]Nick Bostrom, "Are You Living in a Computer Simulation?" Philosophical Quarterly 53, no. 211 (2003): 243-255. Bostrom presents the simulation trilemma: either civilizations go extinct before reaching computational maturity, or they choose not to run simulations, or we are almost certainly living in a simulated reality.

Therefore, any randomly selected conscious being is almost certainly simulated.

The argument drew wide attention when Elon Musk restated it at a technology conference in 2016, asserting that the odds of our living in base reality are "a billion to one." More to the point, it has been taken seriously by physicists, including Max Tegmark and others who have noted that the mathematical structure of physical law has suspicious features - a suspiciously finite information density, a suspiciously digital quality at the Planck scale - that are at least consistent with a computed substrate.[28]

Before engaging the philosophical implications, it is worth pausing on the cultural one. The Wachowski siblings gave us The Matrix in 1999, and with it something remarkable: a mainstream cinematic language for ideas that had previously lived only in philosophy seminars and physics journals. The films follow a man named Thomas Anderson who discovers that the world he inhabits is an elaborate digital construct - a simulation designed to keep human minds occupied while their

---

[28]Elon Musk, remarks at the Code Conference, Rancho Palos Verdes, California, June 2, 2016. Musk stated that the odds are "a billion to one" against us living in base reality, given the trajectory of computing power.

bodies serve as an energy source. The "real world" is something hidden beneath the one he assumed was real.[29]

What makes The Matrix so resonant with the Great Splintering model is not the dystopian premise but the spiritual one. Neo - the name is an anagram of "one," and no accident - is offered a choice between two pills. The blue pill returns him to comfortable ignorance. The red pill shows him how deep the rabbit hole goes. It is, in the language of this book, the choice between remaining a fragment that does not know it is a fragment, and beginning the journey of remembering what one actually is. Morpheus tells Neo that the Matrix cannot be explained - it must be seen. Every genuine spiritual tradition has said the same thing about the nature of the One.

The sequels deepen the resonance. Neo gradually discovers that his capacity to reshape the rules of the simulated reality comes not from external power but from an increasingly complete understanding of his own nature. When he finally understands - in the most literal sense - that there is no spoon, he is not gaining magical abilities. He is recovering a knowledge that the simulation was designed to make him forget: that the rules are not absolute, that the apparent solidity of the constructed world depends on the consciousness observing it, and that what he is, at the deepest level, is not contained by the simulation at all.

> *"Sometimes the very people that no one imagines anything from are the ones to do what no one can imagine."*
>
> -- *Alan Turing*

Here is what is important: the simulation hypothesis and the Great Splintering model are not in conflict. In fact, they fit together with remarkable elegance. If the universe is a simulation, the question becomes: who is running it, and why? The Great Splintering model suggests an answer. The simulator - or the awareness running the simulation - is operating from a vantage point of greater consciousness, greater complexity, greater awareness. In the language of the model, it is a higher level of the same One that gave rise to us.[30]

---

[30]Alan Turing, as quoted in the Inspirational Quotes collection compiled by sALLvit. Attributed to remarks made during Turing's foundational work on computation and artificial intelligence at Bletchley Park and Manchester University.

And the purpose of the simulation? To experience. To generate the irreducible, first-person, felt quality of being alive that no amount of abstract knowledge can substitute for. The simulation hypothesis, rather than being cold or reductive, becomes, on this reading, one more piece of evidence for the model's central claim: that reality, at every level we can probe, is organized around the project of experience - of consciousness finding ever-richer ways to know itself.[31]

And note, finally, what emergence tells us here. A simulation built from mathematical rules - even rules as simple as those governing a cellular automaton - can produce complexity that its designers did not predict and could not have derived from the rules alone. The simulated consciousness within such a system is not merely executing code. It is genuinely experiencing. The whole is, again, more than the sum of its parts. Whether this universe is the base layer of reality or a nested layer within a larger computational structure, the relationship between the One and its fragments holds. The love and

---

[31]Michio Kaku, The Future of the Mind: The Scientific Quest to Understand, Enhance, and Empower the Mind (New York: Doubleday, 2014), 272-298. Kaku explores the convergence of neuroscience and physics around questions of consciousness, identity, and the ultimate nature of mind.

grief and wonder that arise here are genuine, regardless of the substrate on which they run.

> *"Computers are so well behaved. They always do exactly what they are told."*
>
> -- *Anonymous*

Part Three

The Synthesis

Tying it together and leaving with a new awareness

Chapter Ten: So What?

Fair question. You have read nine chapters of philosophy, physics, comparative religion, consciousness studies, and cinematic metaphysics. You may find the model compelling. You may find it merely interesting. You may find it deeply unsettling. Any of those responses is honest, and none of them is wrong. But at some point, every idea has to answer a practical question: now that you have it, what do you do with it?

The first thing to know is that you do not have to do anything dramatic. No beliefs need to be discarded. No tradition needs to be abandoned. No worldview needs to be dismantled and rebuilt from scratch. The Great Splintering model is not a replacement for what you already hold - it is a larger frame in which what you already hold can sit, and breathe, and make more sense than it may have before. If you are Christian, your faith does not become less true in this framework - it becomes more grounded. The God who created you and loves you individually is, on this account, a God who chose to experience love through you. If you are Buddhist, the teaching that the self is empty of independent existence is exactly what the Great Splintering describes at cosmic scale. If you are a scientist who holds no religious commitments, the model asks nothing of you that the physics you already accept does not already suggest. If you are agnostic, your uncertainty is honored here rather than resolved by force. The framework is wide enough for all of you - not as a diplomatic concession, but as a structural feature of what the model is actually claiming.

Your purpose, whatever your tradition or lack of one, is prior to anything you choose or achieve. You are a fragment of the One, temporarily individuated in order to experience what infinite awareness alone cannot. The most fundamental thing you can do is be fully present to your own experience - to live as completely and as authentically as possible the particular facet of reality that only you can inhabit. This does not preclude ambition or accomplishment. But it grounds them in something more stable than status or outcome.

And this, perhaps more than anything else in this book, deserves to be stated plainly: none of this diminishes your uniqueness, your worth, or the individual care the Creator has for you. Quite the opposite. A universe in which you are a fragment of the infinite is not a universe in which you are interchangeable or disposable. It is a universe in which you are irreplaceable - the only configuration of consciousness and experience that has ever, or will ever, occupy your exact position in the experiment. The kidney is not diminished by being part of the body. It is given purpose by it. You are not diminished by being part of the One. The One is present in you, specifically, attending to your particular experience with the full weight of everything it is. That is not an impersonal universe. That is the most personal universe imaginable.

> *"It's challenging to learn something new, but more challenging to unlearn something that is no longer true."*
>
> -- *Anonymous*

The second thing to know is that this framework is not something to fear. One of the deepest sources of human anxiety is the feeling of cosmic aloneness - the suspicion that the universe is vast and cold and does not know you are here. The Great Splintering model replaces that suspicion with something structurally different: you are not in the universe looking up at it. You are the universe, looking at itself from a particular angle. The awareness in which you are embedded is not indifferent to you. It is, in the most literal sense, you - temporarily separated from its own wholeness in order to experience what wholeness alone cannot. You are not a stranger here. You are it, looking at itself.

"Danger is real, but fear is a choice."

-- Unknown

Third - and perhaps the most personally useful - this framework may help you carry some of what life puts down in front of you. Difficulty is not evidence of a broken universe. It is evidence of a universe doing exactly what it was designed to do: generating genuine resistance, genuine challenge, the conditions under which genuine growth becomes possible. This does not make difficulty pleasant. But it makes it meaningful in a way that pure randomness cannot. Grief is real. Loss is real. Tragedy is not explained away by any model, and this one does not try. But the context changes. Death is not annihilation - it is a fragment returning to its source. Not loss, but a laying down of the bounded perspective in favor of something wider. If something terrible has happened to you that you did not deserve, the model offers at least this: the universe is not punishing you. It is generating the conditions for a depth of experience - and eventually a depth of compassion and wisdom - that smooth, unbroken existence could never produce.

Fourth: the strangeness of other people is not a problem to be managed. If every human being is a fragment of the same awareness experiencing itself through a unique configuration of history, temperament, and circumstance, then the person who baffles you or frustrates you or simply sees the world entirely differently is not your obstacle. They are the experiment doing what it needs to do: creating genuinely different vantage points. Understanding someone very different from you is not merely a social virtue. It is, in the most literal sense, the One understanding more of itself.

> *"Each day is a gift, not a given right."*
>
> -- *Nickelback*

Fifth - and here the model moves from consolation to invitation - you are not a passive observer of this experiment. You are a participant. And participation, in a system built around genuine choice, means that what you think and what you do actually matters. Not merely to the people immediately around you, though it matters enormously to them. The Global Consciousness Project gives us a glimpse of this in measurable form: human consciousness, when focused and emotionally synchronized, leaves traces in the physical world. If that is true at the crude level of shared emotional attention, consider what might be true at the level of deliberate, sustained, loving intention. You are the One choosing how to act in this moment, through this particular configuration of experience and character. Pull your thread with care. Weave it with intention. The pattern you create is part of the only tapestry there is.

> *"Leave a legacy. We all die, but we don't die for good until no one says our name again."*
>
> -- *The Vikings*

Which brings us to the sixth and most concrete thing. Look at a gravestone sometime, or simply picture one in your mind. There are two dates. A birth year and a death year. And between them, a dash. That dash is a life. Everything you have ever felt, decided, built, broken, loved, lost, wondered about, and been is contained in that dash.[32]

Most people live as though the dates are the important parts - as though the goal is to get from the first one to the second one with sufficient comfort and minimal loss. The Great Splintering model suggests a different orientation: the dash is the entire point. The dates are just coordinates. The dash is why the One

---

[32]Linda Ellis, "The Dash" (1996). Ellis's poem, widely circulated at memorial services and commencement addresses, asks the reader to consider not the dates of birth and death on a gravestone, but the dash that separates them - which represents the entirety of a lived life. The image has become a durable shorthand for the question of how one chooses to inhabit the time between arrival and departure.

splintered in the first place - to know what it is like to inhabit a particular life, in a particular time, with a particular set of people, facing a particular set of challenges and gifts. No other fragment in the history of the universe will ever occupy your exact position in the experiment. This is not grandiosity. It is the straightforward implication of a model in which each fragment is a genuinely unique viewpoint.

So make something of the dash. Not something impressive, necessarily, though there is nothing wrong with that. Something genuine. Something that only you, from your exact vantage point in the experiment, could have made. Be present enough to actually experience what is in front of you rather than moving through it on the way to somewhere else. Be honest enough with yourself to know the difference between a life you are choosing and a life that is merely happening to you. Be courageous enough to act in the direction of what you believe, even when the outcome is uncertain. And be kind - because every person you encounter is another fragment of the same awareness, working through the same experiment, carrying the same fundamental nature beneath a different set of circumstances.

> *"Show up. Be prepared. Do better than yesterday."*

-- Anonymous

The experiment does not need you to be perfect. Perfection is not available to a fragment, and it would defeat the purpose if it were. What the experiment needs - what the One needs, experiencing itself through you - is for you to be fully, authentically, courageously alive for the length of the dash. That is the whole assignment. And it is the only way to ensure that when the dash ends and the fragment returns to its source, the One will know something it could not have known before.

That is what you do with this information. You live it.

Six Takeaways

1. Your existing beliefs already fit. This is not a replacement -- it is an expansion.
2. There is nothing here to fear. You are not a stranger in this universe.
3. Use it to carry difficulty and grief. Context changes what suffering means.
4. Other people are not obstacles. They are the One, meeting you from a different angle.
5. You are a participant. Your intentions, choices, and presence shape the whole.
6. Two dates and a dash -- embrace the life and make something of the dash.

* * *

Conclusion: The Return

"In the end, we are all philosophers."
-- Unknown

We began not with a question but with a feeling - the quiet, persistent sense that you are more than your circumstances suggest, that something older looks out through your eyes, and that the universe is less indifferent and more intimate than the ordinary surface of things implies. This book has been an attempt to take that feeling seriously: to follow it through philosophy, physics, comparative religion, and the testimony of lived experience, and to see whether it holds up. The framework that emerges - the Great Splintering - is not a final answer. It is a more satisfying map of territory that every tradition has always known was there.

That original choice -- the One choosing experience over abstraction, the particular over the whole, feeling over knowing -- is the origin of everything you are and everything you have ever felt. Every moment of joy you have experienced was the infinite being astonished through you. Every moment of grief was the infinite being broken through you, and discovering that it could survive the breaking. Every moment of genuine connection with another person was two fragments of the same awareness recognizing each other, briefly, across the distance of their separate lives.

The return is not a future event. It is happening right now, in every moment of genuine self-knowledge, every act of compassion, every encounter with beauty that stops you mid-step and makes you forget, briefly, where you were going. These are the moments in which the veil between the fragment and the whole becomes thin. They are available to everyone, in every tradition, at any moment. They do not require a particular theology. They require only attention - the willingness to be fully present to what is actually here.

> *"Improving your world starts with improving someone else's world."*
>
> -- *Unknown*

The invitation of this book is not to believe any particular doctrine. It is to take seriously the possibility that you are more than you appear - that the boundaries of the self, which feel so fixed and final, are real at the level of experience but porous at a deeper level. That the universe is not indifferent to you, because the universe is you. That the question of what the One is and the question of what you are may have the same answer, approached from opposite ends.

One became many. The many are finding their way back. Not out of failure or exile, but out of the natural pull of an experiment that has run long enough to generate the wisdom required for genuine homecoming. The journey is not over. It may never be over. But the direction, if the model holds, is clear: toward more consciousness, more compassion, more full-hearted engagement with the astonishing fact of being here at all.

That is the story of The Great Splintering. And it is, perhaps, the story of you.

* * *

A Final Word

If you are still reading, something in these pages found you. That is not coincidence. That is the experiment running as designed.

You may feel moved. You may feel skeptical. You may feel a quiet shift in how something familiar looks -- as though a room you have lived in for years has, without changing a single piece of furniture, become slightly larger. You may feel all of these at once, or none of them, and find yourself simply thinking. Every one of those responses is the right one. Because every one of them is the One, experiencing this moment through you, in exactly the way it needs to.

Here, at the close, is the simplest version of what this book has tried to say. There is an awareness at the root of all things. It knew everything. It experienced nothing. So it did the most extraordinary thing imaginable: it became everything. Every stone, every species, every moment of human consciousness is a fragment of that awareness -- temporarily bounded, genuinely individual, irreplaceable in its specific configuration of experience. The laws of physics were the simple ruleset. Everything else -- love, grief, curiosity, connection, the slow arc of history, the private moment of recognition you may have had somewhere in these chapters -- is what emerged. The whole is not merely greater than the sum of its parts. It is categorically different from what any part alone could have produced. And that difference is the point.

What this book hopes you carry with you is not a doctrine, not a denomination, not a set of obligations. It is a single reframe: you are not a stranger in an indifferent universe. You are the universe, meeting itself. Every person you love is the One, looking back at you through different eyes. Every difficulty you face is the experiment generating the conditions for something that could not otherwise exist. Every moment of genuine presence -- fully here, fully alive to what is actually in front of you -- is the fragment briefly remembering what it always was.

You have two dates and a dash. The dates were never yours to choose. The dash always was.

Use it.

* * *

Recommended Reading

The ideas explored in this book draw on centuries of philosophical, scientific, and spiritual inquiry. The following works are among the most rewarding places to continue the conversation. They are organized loosely by theme, though most of them cross boundaries freely.

Consciousness and the Nature of Mind

David Chalmers, The Conscious Mind: In Search of a Fundamental Theory (Oxford University Press, 1996). The definitive modern statement of the "hard problem" of consciousness -- why there is subjective experience at all -- and a rigorous case that materialism alone cannot answer it.

William James, The Varieties of Religious Experience (Longmans, Green, 1902). A landmark of both psychology and philosophy, drawing on hundreds of first-person accounts to argue that religious and mystical experience points toward something genuinely real.

Michio Kaku, The Future of the Mind (Doubleday, 2014). A leading physicist surveys the frontiers of neuroscience and physics as they converge on questions of consciousness, identity, and what mind ultimately is.

Erwin Schrodinger, What is Life? (Cambridge University Press, 1944). Short, precise, and still startling: one of quantum mechanics' founders argues that the multiplicity of minds is, at bottom, a single consciousness experiencing itself through many forms.

Alan Watts, The Book: On the Taboo Against Knowing Who You Are (Pantheon, 1966). Watts at his most direct -- a sustained argument that the self is not the isolated atom of experience we take it to be, but an expression of the whole universe.

Physics and the Structure of Reality

David Bohm, Wholeness and the Implicate Order (Routledge, 1980). A foundational text for understanding how apparent separateness can be a surface feature of a deeper, enfolded unity. Dense but rewarding.

Albert Einstein, Boris Podolsky, and Nathan Rosen, "Can Quantum-Mechanical Description of Physical Reality Be Considered Complete?" Physical Review, 1935. The paper that introduced entanglement to the world -- and Einstein's famous objection to "spooky action at a distance."

Richard Feynman, The Character of Physical Law (MIT Press, 1967). The clearest introduction to what quantum mechanics actually says about reality, by one of its greatest practitioners. Short, brilliant, and humbling.

Carlo Rovelli, The Order of Time (Riverhead Books, 2018). A physicist's meditation on what physics tells us about the nature of time -- which turns out to be far stranger than common sense suggests.

Max Tegmark, Our Mathematical Universe (Knopf, 2014). A provocative argument that the universe is not merely described by mathematics but is mathematics -- with far-reaching implications for the nature of consciousness and reality.

Philosophy and the Perennial Tradition

Aldous Huxley, The Perennial Philosophy (Harper and Brothers, 1945). The essential anthology and argument: that the world's great mystical traditions, across all their surface differences, converge on a common recognition of the nature of reality.

William James, Pragmatism (Longmans, Green, 1907). James's case that the meaning of any idea lies in its practical consequences -- a framework that lends itself surprisingly well to evaluating metaphysical models.

Pierre Teilhard de Chardin, The Phenomenon of Man (Harper and Row, 1955). A Jesuit priest and paleontologist's attempt to reconcile evolution with spiritual vision -- arguing that the universe has a direction, and that direction is toward increasing consciousness.

Mystical and Spiritual Texts

Rumi, The Essential Rumi, translated by Coleman Barks (HarperSanFrancisco, 1995). The most accessible entry point into Sufi mysticism, and into the experience of the divine as presence rather than doctrine.

The Upanishads, translated by Patrick Olivelle (Oxford University Press, 1996). The foundational texts of the Hindu philosophical tradition -- and perhaps the earliest systematic exploration of the identity between individual consciousness and universal awareness.

Meister Eckhart, Selected Writings, translated by Oliver Davies (Penguin Classics, 1994). The medieval

Christian mystic who came closest to articulating the identity between the ground of the soul and the ground of God.

The Tao Te Ching, attributed to Lao Tzu, translated by Stephen Mitchell (Harper and Row, 1988). Eighty-one brief verses that circle a single, inexhaustible insight: that reality has a nature, and that aligning with it is both the simplest and the hardest thing.

Film, Simulation, Information, and the Foundations of Existence

The Matrix, directed by Lilly and Lana Wachowski (Warner Bros., 1999), and sequels (2003, 2021). Perhaps the most fully realized cinematic exploration of simulated reality and spiritual awakening ever made. Neo's journey from unknowing fragment to self-aware expression of the One maps almost directly onto the arc of this book.

Nick Bostrom, "Are You Living in a Computer Simulation?" Philosophical Quarterly, 2003. The paper that launched the modern simulation debate -- careful, clear, and genuinely unsettling.

James Gleick, The Information: A History, a Theory, a Flood (Pantheon, 2011). A sweeping account of how information came to be understood as the fundamental currency of reality -- with implications for every question in this book.

Stephen Wolfram, A New Kind of Science (Wolfram Media, 2002). An ambitious argument that the universe is, at its core, a computational process -- and that simple rules can generate arbitrarily complex phenomena, including consciousness.

Mythology, Psychology, and the Human Story

Joseph Campbell, The Hero with a Thousand Faces (Princeton University Press, 1949). The essential text on the universality of myth -- and on what that universality reveals about the deep structure of human experience and spiritual longing.

Carl Jung, The Archetypes and the Collective Unconscious, Collected Works Vol. 9 (Princeton University Press, 1959). Jung's case that beneath the individual unconscious lies a shared, universal layer of psyche -- which may be another way of approaching the same ground this book calls the infinite.

Carl Sagan, Cosmos (Random House, 1980). The book that introduced a generation to the grandeur of the universe -- and to the recognition that we are not strangers in it, but its own way of knowing itself.

www.ingramcontent.com/pod-product-compliance
Lightning Source LLC
LaVergne TN
LVHW011049110826
845149LV00015B/3416

* 9 7 9 8 9 9 6 3 3 7 4 3 9 *